Cowboy's Big Dream

Thank you for lending
a paw to SMSD
& our veterans!
♡ - Haylee Schubel

PAGE PUBLISHING
Conneaut Lake, PA

First originally published by Page Publishing 2022

ISBN 978-1-6624-7884-0 (hc)
ISBN 978-1-6624-7883-3 (digital)

Printed in the United States of America

Cowboy's Big Dream

HAYLEE SCHWEIBEL

Based on a true story.

When Cowboy was a puppy, he had
big dreams. He didn't understand what
these big dreams were about, just that
in the dreams, he was so happy.
He was raised by a foster family who
had him for fifteen months. During
that time, he learned lots of things.

2

These were some things
NOT to do: nipping
and biting fingers,

3

chewing on furniture, peeing in the house,

stealing stuff (like the kitchen towels).

4

He learned to never eat food off the
floor or counters (that's really bad!)
and especially NOT to chase the cat.

He learned a lot of fun things too:
sit, lie down, wait,
and how to put on a vest.

He learned to walk beside people and not pull on the leash. Cowboy even learned to use his nose to close drawers and doors, to bring things without chewing on them, and even to go to stores and restaurants.

Cowboy got lots of yummy
treats when he did all of these
things, which he loved!

9

Not everything was easy, though. You see, he loved people and other dogs. Cowboy had to ignore everything going on around him and only pay attention to his trainer. It didn't take long for him to realize that if he focused on his trainer, he got lots of treats.

Cowboy also got lots of love and was just like any other dog. He spent time watching TV, playing fetch and tug-of-war, taking walks and car rides, and playing with other dogs. He especially loved anything to do with water like swimming, paddleboarding, and boating.

He even played dress
up on holidays.

Cowboy's favorite thing was playing fetch
with tennis balls, but he loved naps and
dreaming a big dream most of all!

When Cowboy got older, it was time to go to college. He still got to see his foster family on weekends or was able to visit other families. He loved college and his trainers. He always enjoyed learning new things and he still got lots of treats! Cowboy learned to be around wheelchairs and walkers and how to bring bigger items to people like canes or laundry baskets. A tricky thing to learn was picking up a credit card off the floor!

By the end of each day, he was always tired and happy to go to sleep and dream his big dream.

After about six
months of being
in college, it was
time to stay with a new
foster family to await his
big dream, whatever that was.

17

When Cowboy turned about
two and a half years old,
he finally got to meet
someone. This someone
was just perfect for him in every
way possible! Cowboy knew exactly
what this someone needed: a dog
like him to help make life a little
easier and, most importantly,
to just be a companion.

Now it was time for Cowboy to take the test. He had to show he learned his commands and could ignore everything. Cowboy loved bringing his companion things and walking next to him to help for balance. He would do anything he could to help, especially wear his special harness.

Luckily Cowboy passed the test!

Cowboy was certified as a service dog for a veteran, and they had a big celebration they call Passing of the Leash.

He got to greet everyone that worked with him as they passed his leash from one person to the next. He even got to see his foster family.

After seeing everyone, Cowboy finally got to his favorite person, his new companion.

It didn't take long for Cowboy to realize that helping his companion was what he had always been dreaming about. Being with his companion was his big dream, and nothing made him happier.

Smoky Mountain Service Dogs

- Mission is to enhance the physical and psychological quality of life for wounded veterans by providing custom-trained mobility assistance service dogs (at no cost to the veteran).
- Has only five paid employees (four professional canine trainers and a facilities manager).
- Has two hundred dedicated volunteers, including the Board of Directors. Our volunteers raise our puppies, socialize and provide respite and foster care for our dogs in training, transport our dogs for training and veterinary visits, attend community events, keep our books, mow our lawn, and even make our dog vests. This business model allows ninety-five cents of every donated dollar to go directly to the care and training of our canines.
- Has trained and paired over fifty highly skilled service dogs with deserving veterans as of the date of this publication.
- Is accredited by Assistance Dogs International, the internationally recognized leader of assistance dogs standards. This validates that the facilities and operation of the SMSD program meets or exceeds ADI standards.

Please visit
www.smokymountainservicedogs.org
for more information on how to make a donation
or to learn about our volunteer opportunities.

25

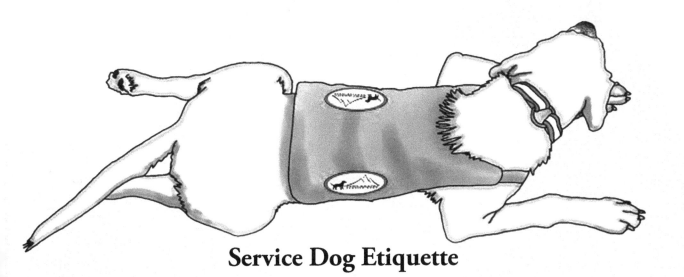

Service Dog Etiquette

Do not interact with the dog in any way. Examples of poor etiquette that should not happen when one sees a service animal are:

- talking, whistling, cooing, or barking at the animal
- petting or asking to pet
- praising the pet when it completes its task
- tapping your leg or clapping your hands
- allowing your children to approach
- speaking to the handler, saying things such as:

  "What is wrong with you?"

  "What a good dog you have!"

  "What happened?"

  "What is his name?"

  "I have a friend that fosters service dogs."

  "I know you are not supposed to pet, but I just can't resist!"

- asking for a demonstration

The American Valor Foundation is proud to be a sustaining partner of Smoky Mountain Service Dogs, and we're honored to name service dog Cowboy in HONOR and MEMORY of our son and brother, SOC (SEAL) Chris Kyle, United States Navy.

I would like to thank the Kyle family and Smoky Mountain Service Dogs for Cowboy; he has been a godsend. Cowboy assists me with my mobility and picking up and retrieving items. Cowboy is my constant companion and is always by my side to provide me emotional support.

MSgt. Paul Miles, USMC Ret.

About the Author

Haylee Schweibel has a bachelor's degree in Visual Communication of Fine Arts from Ball State University. She is an avid artist who loves working with her hands dabbling with any medium. She loves anything with nature and gardening. With her growing interest in animals and their behaviors, she has been a volunteer with Smoky Mountain Service Dogs (SMSD) since 2018 as a puppy raiser. Haylee's first puppy was Cowboy. She felt compelled to share her rewarding experience with others. Duke and Winston are currently awaiting their veteran to fulfill their big dream. She is currently raising her fourth puppy for SMSD, Henley; with her husband, Brad; their dog, Guinness; and a cat, Arkie.

CPSIA information can be obtained
at www.ICGtesting.com
Printed in the USA
LVHW071906011222
733367LV00002B/7